55 Years of

LONG
BEACH
ISLAND

BEACH
BADGES

1967-2022

DOWN THE SHORE
PUBLISHING
West Creek, New Jersey

55 Years of
LONG BEACH ISLAND
BEACH BADGES
1967-2022

Down The Shore Publishing / Down The Shore Books LLC
PO Box 100, West Creek, NJ 08092
www.down-the-shore.com
The words "Down The Shore" and Down The Shore logo are a registered U.S. Trademark.

Book Design by Leslee Ganss

First edition, 2023
Printed in China
10 9 8 7 6 5 4 3 2 1

Library of Congress Cataloging-in-Publication Data

Names: Kugel, Robert, 1957- author.
Title: 55 years of Long Beach Island beach badges : 1967-2022 / Robert
Kugel.
Other titles: Fifty-five years of Long Beach Island beach badges, 1967-2022

Description: First edition. | West Creek, New Jersey : Down The Shore
Publishing, 2023.
Identifiers: LCCN 2023004466 | ISBN 9781593221416 (hardcover)
Subjects: LCSH: Long Beach Island (N.J.)--Miscellanea. | Badges--New
Jersey. | Beaches--New Jersey--Long Beach Island.
Classification: LCC F142.L65 .K844 2023 | DDC
974.9/48043--dc23/eng/20230208
LC record available at https://lccn.loc.gov/2023004466

ISBN 978-1-59322-141-6

"Badges?
We Don't Need No
Stinking Badges!"

(Well, as long as you're
not in New Jersey)

Contents

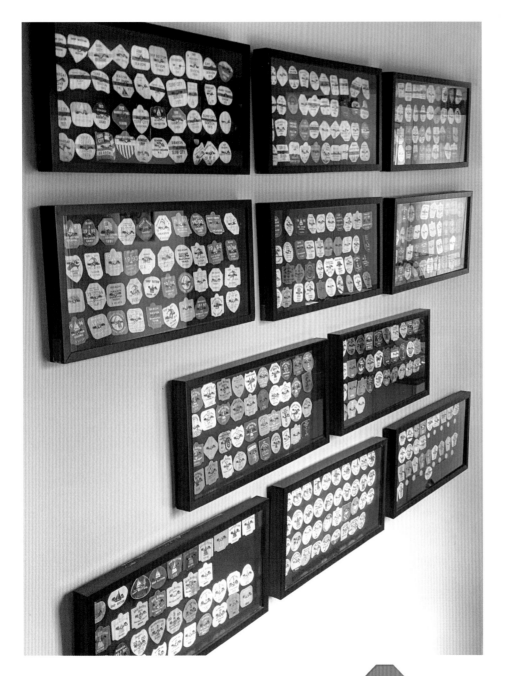

Preface
You Collect What?

I purchased my Ship Bottom house in 1984. In Ship Bottom, like the other five towns on Long Beach Island, if I want to go to the beach in the summer I need to have a beach badge. And so every May I go to borough hall and purchase eight seasonal beach badges. Although I don't remember the cost those first few years I do recall purchasing eight badges in 1987 for $64. (The cost in 2022: $280)

At the end of each year I'd put them in a plastic bag and keep these now-expired badges in the closet. The routine went on for 20 years or so. Every now and then I'd take the badges out to look at them — it always brought back fond memories of past summers with family and friends — and then back in the closet they went. A few times, I asked myself why I was saving them. At one point, instead of keeping all eight from each year, I even threw out four of the eight from every year I had kept to that point. But I just couldn't bring myself to throw them all away.

One day when I had them out of the closet, it occurred to me that it would be nice to display them in a shadowbox in my home. Soon after that I decided I'd try to find and collect every seasonal badge that had been issued by Ship Bottom. I purchased a lot on eBay, found many at yard sales, and some I obtained from people who heard of my quest.

But I had also acquired a few seasonal badges from Surf City, and before I knew it I was collecting badges from all six townships on Long Beach Island.

The seasonal badges consist of all badges from the first year issued to 2022. In the summer 2021, I acquired the last missing badge to complete my collection of LBI seasonal beach badges — Surf City's 1968 seasonal badge.

Over the years I have expanded my collection to include daily, weekly, senior, holiday, and specialty badges as well. These badges are more of a challenge to find as most people only hang on to the seasonal badges.

Over time I've met many collectors of beach badges. However, unlike me, most people only collect seasonal badges from one specific town on the Island.

This may be the largest overall LBI collection, with more than 800 badges — a combination of seasonal, weekly, daily, holiday and specialty badges.

In this book, the holiday badges consist of 45 of the 62 limited edition badges issued since 2011. The weekly and daily badges — the largest part of the collection — also have the biggest gaps and missing badges. For the senior badges, only a few are missing, (mostly Harvey Cedars and a few Barnegat Light). The specialty badges consist of a dozen or so — a few not even LBI-related. I purchased these if it was something unusual.

Many people see previous beach badges and associate them with events in their lives. Kris Kain of Ship Bottom remembers the 2017 seasonal badge vividly as the year the color matched her bathing suit perfectly. For most people, a beach badge might be associated with an event such as the year they were married, met their spouse, purchased their home on LBI, or — frequently — the year a child was born.

I have met many people through the "LBI Beach Badge Collectors" Facebook page (with over 1100 members as of late 2022) where I bought, sold, and swapped badges, as well as shared stories, and helped others find missing badges to complete their collections.

My favorites? While I think Harvey Cedars has released some very creative and artsy badges for the last 40 years, I have three badges I always point out when showing off my collection: Harvey Cedars's 2007 seasonal badge that sports a cool pair of summery flip flops; Long Beach Township's 2006 complementary Starbucks daily badge; Ship Bottom's 2009 handicap badge (the last two mainly because they are so unusual).

Beach Badges on LBI And in New Jersey

If you're from anywhere but New Jersey, most likely you don't even know what a beach badge is.

Of the 50 states that make up the United States, 23 are on a coastline along the ocean and 8 states that border a coastline are on one of the Great Lakes. (New York is on both lists.) Only New Jersey — *yes, only New Jersey* — requires that in most towns along the shore, in the summer season, you must pay a fee to get on the beach. Why, you ask? Because this is Jersey and that's the way we roll. In New Jersey, nothing is free, baby, or so it seems.

A 1930 brass "bathing privilege" badge for Avon-by-the Sea, and one of the earliest plastic badges for Avon in 1941.

Municipal beach badges were first required in Bradley Beach, in Monmouth County in 1929. Many other oceanfront towns in New Jersey jumped on the bandwagon during the 1940s and 1950s. Some of the earliest badges were made of brass or tin and plastic badges started to appear in the early 1940s.

There are some New Jersey towns along the Delaware Bay and Raritan Bay that do not require a fee for beach access. And Atlantic City, Wildwood, Wildwood Crest, North Wildwood, and Strathmere are oceanfront towns that still offer free beaches.

Depending on where you are on the Jersey shore that piece of plastic pinned to your bathing suit may be referred to as a "beach badge," a "beach tag," or in rare instances (Long Branch) a "beach pass."

The phrase "beach badge" is used here on Long Beach Island and as far north as Sea Bright. However, south of LBI, starting in Brigantine and to the southern tip of Cape May Point, those little pieces of plastic are referred to as "beach tags."

It's unclear why different names evolved in shore lingo. Perhaps it's a Philadelphia-South Jersey / New York-North

Jersey distinction. Or maybe like Taylor Ham and pork roll. Or Bennies and Shoobies, jimmies and sprinkles.

The first Long Beach Island communities to require a fee to access the beach in the summer season were Surf City and Ship Bottom in 1967. A decade later all LBI towns were issuing badges; Beach Haven was the last to require badges in 1978. The user fee was presented as a way offset the expense of maintaining the beach, equipment, and paying lifeguards and badge checkers.

LBI REQUIREMENTS AND SALES

On Long Beach Island, beach badges are required from mid-June until Labor Day. Each municipality (Barnegat Light, Harvey Cedars, Surf City, Ship Bottom, Long Beach Township and Beach Haven) follows the same seasonal schedule. Badges are available in all six town's municipal offices from early May until Labor Day.

Pre-season discounted seasonal badges are offered in all towns (the cutoff dates for the discounted price vary from town to town, between May 31 to June 15).

Weekly and daily badges can usually be purchased on the beach as well as at a location designated by the town.

Ship Bottom, Harvey Cedars, Barnegat Light and Beach Haven offer beach badge sales on the internet with an app called "Viply." (viplypass.com), however there is no shipping of orders. With online purchases you still have to pick the badges up in person.

All LBI towns offer discounted badges for senior citizens who are age 65 and over, and free badges — or free beach access without a badge — for veterans and active duty military personel with proper ID.

Both Bradley Beach and Avon-by-the-Sea issued badges by gender (which made it harder to share badges). A metal beach badge in Lavallette, like the 1999 senior badge above, got so hot in the summer sun that it caused a burn on a beachgoer; the metal badges were discontinued.

Badges valid for an entire season have alternately displayed "Season" and "Seasonal" depending on the year and town (although sometimes neither word is used on the badge).

Some towns have added the phrase "No Refunds No Returns" to badges. Why would beachgoers try to return badges? Often because they bought badges for the wrong town; or want to return them after their vacation is over; or purchased more then they need; or wanted to return badges due to inclement weather (more often for daily badges). Buyer beware!

All towns, except Harvey Cedars, are now issuing badges with serial numbers. These badges are sold in numeric order. These numbers are used in audits and accounting to prove monies received match the badges sold each day, but are not used to track the buyer.

Beach badges are not cross-honored from town to town. Proposals have surfaced over the years for a single badge honored throughout the island (either in addition to, or to replace the town badges), but the revenue sharing calculation has always been an impossible challenge. On a few occassions, however, some towns have chosen to honor other LBI town's badges during the last weeks of the summer season.

The hours badges are required on the beach, and the badges available from the checkers, by town:

Town	Hours	Seasonal	Weekly	Daily
Barnegat Light	10-4 sat-sun 9-3:30 m-f	Y	Y	Y
Harvey Cedars	10-3	N	Y	Y
Surf City	10-5	Y	Y	Y
Ship Bottom	10-4	Y	Y	Y
Long Beach Township	10-4	Y	Y	Y
Beach Haven	10-3:30	N	Y	Y

Beach Badge Q & A

Is it true that if you're wearing street clothes you are not required to have a beach badge?

It depends on the town! In Ship Bottom, Harvey Cedars and Surf City no badge is required when in street clothes. Same in Beach Haven and Long Beach Township "except when any individual so attired utilizes said beaches, bathing or recreational areas for swimming, sunbathing or other recreational purposes." (Don't swim in your street clothes!) In Barnegat Light, however, the code book offers no exceptions. (Apparently you should attach a beach badge to your suit and tie or fancy dress.)

How are confrontations with badge checkers handled?

If a beach badge checker encounters someone who refuses to show or purchase a beach badge, the situation is referred to the badge supervisor.

If not resolved by the badge supervisor, it's referred to lifeguard supervisor. If not resolved by the lifeguard supervisor, it's referred to the police.

In a few instances, belligerent beachgoers have faced court appearances and fines. (These are the procedures in Ship Bottom, Harvey Cedars, and the township.)

How do people try to avoid the beach badge checkers or buying a beach badge:
- Go in the water when the checker comes along.
- Take a walk on the beach when they see the checker.
- Pretend they're sleeping when the checker comes by.
- Go to the beach before 10 am and after 4 or 5 pm when the checkers leave for the day.
- Mix in a few expired badges from previous years, whether they be on their beach bag, chair, or when they are in a zip lock bag.

Favorite excuses people use when they don't have a beach badge:
- My mom has all the badges.
- It's on my other bathing suit.
- I only have hundred-dollar bills.
- I live here year round.
- I'm a taxpayer!
- I forgot it, it's at the house.
- It's on my chair/blanket 'over there.'
- My friends on the beach have badges for me.

Are badge collectors a large group beyond LBI? Are they scattered around the country or mostly in NJ?

There are people collecting New Jersey beach badges across the country but most are in the New Jersey, New York, and Pennsylvania region. Facebook has at least four or five pages dedicated to beach badges. The "LBI Beach Badge Collectors" is the largest, followed by "Lavallette Beach Badges."

Are there any deals or discounts on LBI beach badges?

Senior citizen badges are relatively cheap (and once were free). If you're a veteran or active duty military, you have beach privileges either with a free badge or by showing ID. Everybody else can get a pre-season discount on season badges (different sale dates for each town). And the special holiday badges, often bought as stocking stuffers, actually work as valid badges for the next summer.

Surf City

Beach Badges

Surf City

Seasonal Badges

Surf City was the first town on Long Beach Island to require beach badges. In 1966, the borough council decided that for the following summer, beachgoers would be required to purchase a beach badge to help offset the cost of beach upkeep.

Surf City's seasonal badges from 1967 to 1987 had a pretty generic look, with a change in shape, color, and year — the early badges simply said "Surf City Season" and later a year. The exception was 1976, the year of the American Bicentennial, when the borough issued a waving red, white and blue flag badge with "Surf City" in the blue square instead of the flag's stars.

Although the town did change the shape and color between that first summer of 1967 and 1969, the seasonal badge did not include the year the badge was valid for until 1970. Surf City's classic surfer silloutte was introduced in 1993 and was featured every year until 2009.

In 1988, seasonal beach badges were issued with serial numbers to track inventory and prove monies received match the badges sold each day.

Since 2010, the classic surfer has been replaced with other shore images. In 2017 and 2018 a different surfer appeared on the badges — this one standing, holding a surfboard in silloutte. The disclaimer "No Refunds – No Returns" began appearing on all the borough's badges in 2015. The full phrase only appeared on seasonal badges; "No Returns" appeared on weekly and daily badges.

1967-1978

Seasonal 1979-1990

1991-2002

SURF CITY
1991
SEASON
011583

SURF CITY
19 92
SEASON
A 007246

SURF CITY
19 93
SEASON
R 022908

SURF CITY
19 94
SEASON
A 004930

SURF CITY
19 95
SEASON
A 010256

SURF CITY
19 96
SEASON
A 006485

SURF CITY
19 97
SEASON
006912

SURF CITY
19 98
SEASON
010314

SURF CITY
19 99
SEASON
002268

SURF CITY
2000
SEASON
006406

SURF CITY
2001
Seasonal
008955

SURF CITY
2002
Seasonal
009219

Seasonal 2003-2014

2015-2022

SURF CITY
SEASONAL 2015
No Refunds - No Returns
5303

SURF CITY
SEASONAL 2016
No Refunds - No Returns
9645

SURF CITY
SEASONAL 2017
No Refunds - No Returns
01274

SURF CITY
SEASONAL 2018
No Refunds - No Returns
00142

SURF CITY
SEASONAL 2019
No Refunds - No Returns
03865

SURF CITY
SEASONAL 2020
No Refunds - No Returns
14701

SURF CITY
SEASONAL 2021
No Refunds - No Returns
03748

SURF CITY
SEASONAL 2022
No Refunds - No Returns
02176

Senior Badges

Surf City does not offer beach badges for senior citizens, but admission to the beach is free for those 65 and over with proof of age upon entering the beach.

Veteran/Military Badges

Surf City does not offer veteran or military beach badges, however free access to the beach is given to active military, their immediate family, and veterans with proper ID.

Surf City's beach badge office, rear of Borough Hall, 813 Long Beach Blvd.

1999 SHIP BOTTOM SEASONAL 007861

Ship Bottom

Beach Badges

Ship Bottom

Seasonal Badges

Like Surf City, neighboring Ship Bottom decided that they, too, would impose a charge for the use of the beach. So, for the summer of 1967, beachgoers in Ship Bottom were also required to purchase beach badges. Beachgoers had the option to purchase either a seasonal or weekly badge.

The 1967 season badge simply read "Ship Bottom Season" and there was no year printed on the badge. The year was added on the 1968 badges.

The words "Season" or "Seasonal" were in use on the badges until 2000, but were replaced in 2001 with the phrase "Swim Near A Lifeguard." It's advice that Long Beach Township started printing on their badges five years earlier in 1996. Both Ship Bottom and the township still display that phrase on their seasonal badges. The 1976 American Bicentennial seasonal badge was a red, white and blue shield with only the name "Ship Bottom" printed in the blue field at the top. When the borough celebrated its 75th anniversary, the year 2000 seasonal badge

featured an anchor and reads "75th Anniversary."

In 1971 Ship Bottom began using various images of a sailboat on its badge. It continued the theme until that anniversary summer of 2000 when, after 29 seasons, the sailboat was replaced with the anchor. Both the sailboat and the anchor are symbolic of Ship Bottom's history. In 1983 the anchor of the Italian Bark *Fortuna,*

1967-1978

Seasonal 1979-1990

1991-2002

1991 SHIP BOTTOM SEASONAL A 004812

1992 SHIP BOTTOM SEASONAL A 002019

1993 SHIP BOTTOM SEASONAL A 011062

1994 SHIP BOTTOM SEASONAL A 002395

SHIP BOTTOM SEASONAL 1995

1996 SHIP BOTTOM SEASONAL A 017187

1997 SHIP BOTTOM SEASONAL 001249

1998 SHIP BOTTOM SEASONAL 000838

1999 SHIP BOTTOM SEASONAL 007861

SHIP BOTTOM 2000 75th Anniversary 000243

SHIP BOTTOM 2001 Swim Near A Lifeguard 012823

Ship Bottom 2002 Swim Near A Lifeguard 005632

Seasonal 2003-2014

which wrecked off the 16th Street beach in 1909, was uncovered and salvaged. The ship had long been a symbol for the borough, and the anchor was restored and displayed in front of the borough hall. The partial skeleton still lies under the sand. After storms, when conditions were right, remnants from the *Fortuna*'s decaying keel would become exposed. However, recent beach replenishment projects in which offshore sand is dredged onto the beach have deeply buried the wreck (along with jetties and beach glass).

Typically the shape, color and typeface of badges change annually, to prevent attempts to re-use last year's badge or for beach badge checkers to verify at a quick glance. Although Ship Bottom has changed the colors and typeface on its seasonal badges, the shape has not changed since 1990, except in 1995 (when a different badge manufacturer was used). In 1990, seasonal beach badges were issued with serial numbers for accounting purposes.

Senior Badges

Ship Bottom first offered senior beach badges in 1990. Available to any person 65 or older — and initially free — they were green with a sailboat and white type that read only "Ship Bottom". In 1996 the borough began charging one dollar for the badges and the cost gradually increased over the years. The cost was raised to $10 in 2010 and has remained at that price as of 2022.

Those original green senior badges were valid for life and are still honored today.

Beginning in 2000 new senior beachgoers were required to purchase a senior badge each season. That summer, senior badges were no longer valid for life and were issued only for the year that appeared on the badge.

The shape of the earlier senior badges (1990-1999) changed over the years but the colors stayed the same. In 1995, the senior badge was white with green lettering and a sailboat, when the town changed the company that made the badges for that one season.

Ship Bottom chose to differentiate the senior badges from seasonal badges in 2012 by flip-flopping the badge's background and lettering colors to be opposite of those used on the seasonal badge.

In 2018 Ship Bottom's iconic sailboat was changed to the anchor and the words "Swim Near A Lifeguard" was added — a design change that occurred with seasonal badges back in 2000.

The word "Senior" was added to the badges in 2019 to avoid any confusion between regular seasonal and senior badges,

The original senior badge (left) and the 1995 version.

"Flopped" colors on the 2014 senior badge (left) and the seasonal badge.

Ship Bottom's "good-for-life" senior badges.

Senior 2011-2022

Veteran/Military Badges

Ship Bottom does not offer veteran or military badges. However, beach access is free for veterans and active military (and immediate family) when proper ID is presented to badge checkers.

Handicap Badges

A handicap badge was issued by the borough at no cost to any handicapped person who requested one from 2006 to 2019. Due to misuse and misrepresentation, Ship Bottom discontinued the handicap badge in 2011.

This 1977 Beachcomber photo (left) shows badge checkers, who are identified on the beach by a required blue button-down shirt, a pith helmet and badge identifying them as a "Beach Badge Inspector."

Ship Bottom beach badge checkers rally round their captain (Ed Spataro, seated) after a hard day's work. From left to right — Linda Godfrey, Danny Priff, Marianne Kramer, Tom Parsekian and Lisa Russell.

HEADQUARTERS

SHIP BOTTOM BEACH PATROL

NEW JERSEY

The official badge and pith helmet are no longer used. Over time the uniform became less formal with simple shirts identifying beach badge personnel as a badge checker.

Harvey Cedars

Beach Badges

Harvey Cedars   *Seasonal Badges*

Following in the footsteps of Surf City and Ship Bottom, two years later in the summer of 1969 Harvey Cedars also made the decision to require summer beachgoers to purchase beach badges.

Harvey Cedars' badges, like other neighboring towns, in the early years from 1969 to 1983, were basic in design with only annual changes in color and shape.

But in 1984 Harvey Cedars badges become much more creative and artsy. Each year's new badge displayed something unique and different than the year before. Gone were the years of just a change in shape, type, and color. The badges featured original illustrations of starfish, crabs, turtles, gulls, dunes, beach umbrellas, dolphins, a whale, a lifeguard chair, and the town's Sunset Park pavillion, among other images.

These great designs were provided by various sources; some were created by borough employees, and some created by school children from LBI Elementary School art classes.

The 2002 seasonal badge is the only Harvey Cedars badge issued with serial numbers to date.

1969-1980

997
HARVEY CEDARS
SEASON
1969

HARVEY CEDARS
SEASON
1970

HARVEY CEDARS
SEASON
1971

HARVEY CEDARS
SEASON
1972

1973
HARVEY CEDARS
SEASON

1974
SEASON
HARVEY
CEDARS

HARVEY
CEDARS
SEASON
1975

SEASON
1976
HARVEY CEDARS
N.J.

1977
SEASON
HARVEY CEDARS

1978
SEASON
HARVEY CEDARS

1979
SEASON
HARVEY
CEDARS

HARVEY
CEDARS
SEASON
1980

Seasonal 1981-1992

1993-2004

HARVEY CEDARS 1993 SEASON

Harvey Cedars 1994 Season

HARVEY CEDARS 1995 SEASON

HARVEY CEDARS 1996 SEASON

HARVEY CEDARS 1997 SEASON

HARVEY CEDARS 1998 SEASON

HARVEY CEDARS 1999 SEASON

HARVEY CEDARS 2000 SEASON

BOROUGH OF HARVEY CEDARS OCEAN COUNTY N.J. 20 01 Seasonal

Harvey Cedars Borough of 2002 Ocean County, N.J. Season 005537

Borough of Harvey Cedars 2003 Season Ocean County N.J.

Harvey Cedars 2004

Seasonal 2005-2016

HARVEY CEDARS

20 HC 05

2006 SEASON

HARVEY CEDARS

2007 Season

HARVEY CEDARS

2008 SEASON

HARVEY CEDARS 2009

HARVEY CEDARS

2010

HARVEY CEDARS

2011

HARVEY CEDARS 2012

2013 HARVEY CEDARS

SEASONAL

HARVEY CEDARS SEASONAL

2014

HARVEY CEDARS 2015

SEASONAL

HARVEY CEDARS

2016 SEASONAL

Senior Badges

Harvey Cedars first offered a senior beach badge in 1991 for any beachgoer who was 65 and older at no cost. It was good for life. If you still have one today it is honored. In 1996 "good-for-life" senior badges were no longer offered and the cost was $7. The price gradually increased to $12 by 2022. The first senior badges were identified with the letters S C, for senior citizen. In subsequent years senior badges resembled that years' seasonal badge, except for a change in the color of the type or background, or shape. It was not until 2013 that the word "senior" appeared on the badge, and continues to do so today.

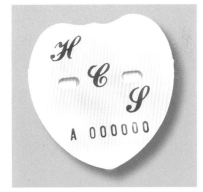

The 1996 Harvey Cedars "good-for-life" senior badge.

Senior Badges 1999-2017

2018-2022

Veteran/Military Badges

Harvey Cedars does not offer veteran or military beach badges; however free access to the beach is available to active military, their immediate family, and veterans with proper ID.

Harvey Cedars beach badge office, Sunset Park, W. Salem Ave., Harvey Cedars.

A 1979 legal notice.

Barnegat Light

Beach Badges

Barnegat Light

Seasonal Badges

Along with Harvey Cedars, the summer of '69 was the year Barnegat Light began to charge for the use of their beaches.

The most recognizable landmark on the Jersey Shore is Barnegat Lighthouse, and the borough has used a lighthouse image on its seasonal badges for 48 of the last 54 seasons. (The lighthouse graphic is generic and often looks nothing like Barnegat Light, but we get the idea!)

Like many of the other towns, Barnegat Light has switched, over the years, between the words "Season" and "Seasonal", while having no designation in the earlier years.

Seasonal badges since 1989 have been issued with serial numbers but, as in other towns, are only used for accounting purposes. Like other LBI towns, Barnegat Light alternates the shape, color and typeface of its badges from year to year, but continues to use a lighthouse as the graphic.

1969-1980

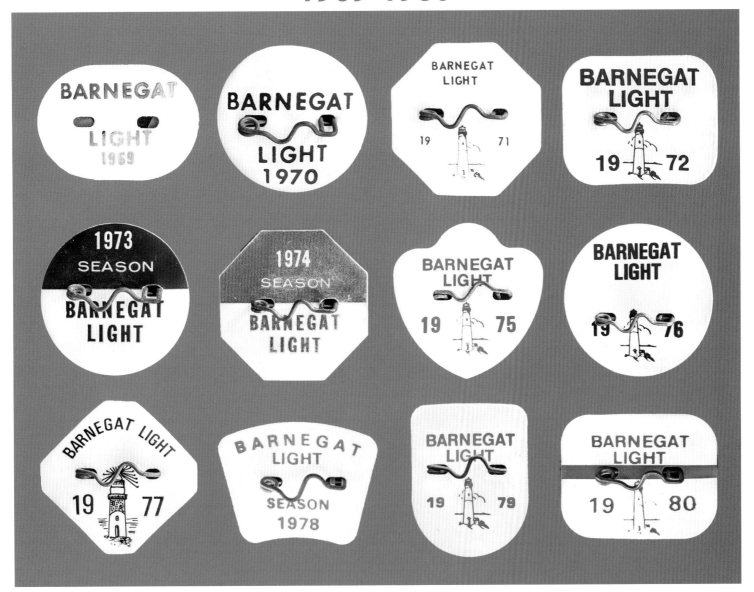

Seasonal 1981-1992

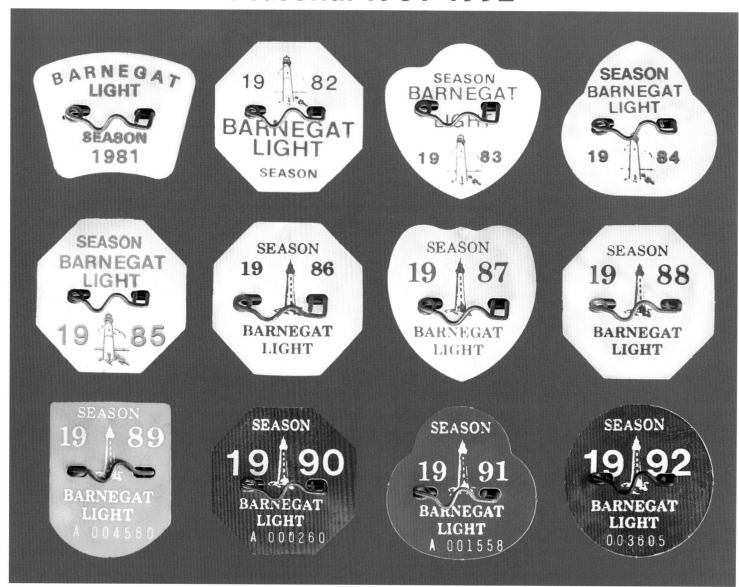

1993-2004

SEASON
19**93**
BARNEGAT
LIGHT
003789

SEASON
19**94**
BARNEGAT
LIGHT
A 003433

SEASON
19**95**
BARNEGAT
LIGHT
A 002724

Season
19 **96**
BARNEGAT LIGHT
006947

Season
19 **97**
BARNEGAT LIGHT
002549

Season
19 **98**
BARNEGAT LIGHT
000570

Season
19 **99**
BARNEGAT LIGHT
004001

Season
20 **00**
BARNEGAT LIGHT
04361

20 **01**
Barnegat Light
Seasonal
001579

20 **02**
Seasonal
Barnegat Light
004217

2003
Barnegat Light
Seasonal
001839

Seasonal
Barnegat Light
2004
006054

Seasonal 2005-2016

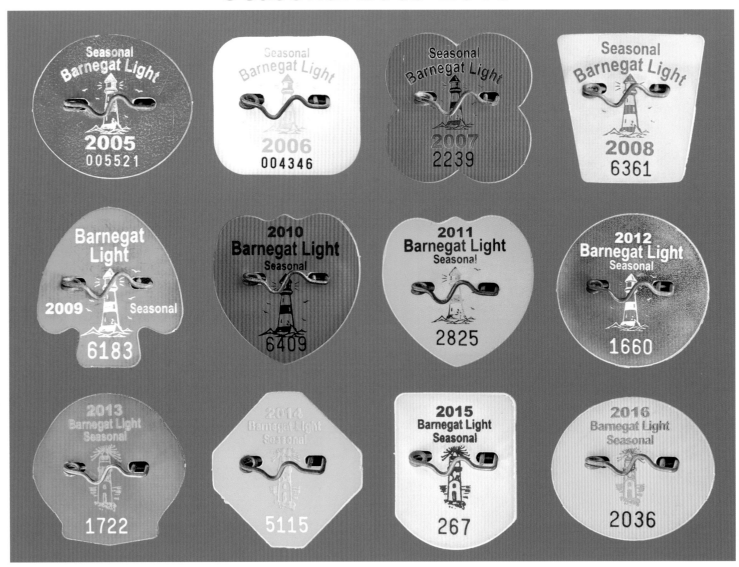

2017-2022

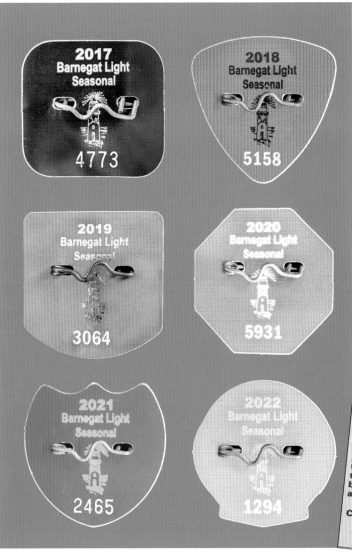

Veteran/Military Badges

On a special free badge available to all veterans, as well as anyone currently serving in the military, "Barnegat Light Thanks You For Your Service." These beach badges were first issued in 2015 and are valid for the current season only, free with proper ID.

A 1979 legal notice.

Barnegat Light beach badge office, 10th Street, Barnegat Light.

Senior Badges 1996-2013

2014-2022

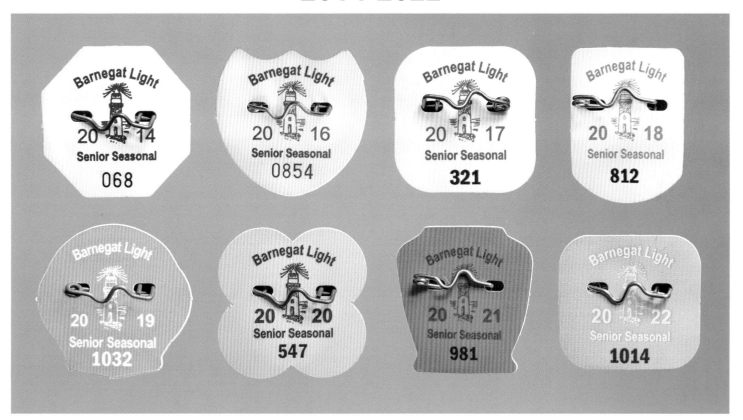

Senior Badges

Barnegat Light's senior beach badges were first issued in 1995. A senior badge could be purchased in 1997 for $7 and the cost has gradually increased to $12 as of 2022.

Like the seasonal badges, Barnegat Light's senior badges alternate in shape and color from year to year, while continuing to use a lighthouse graphic. Only 1995 had the word "Season," 1996 to present reads "Senior Seasonal."

Long Beach Township

Beach Badges

Long Beach Township
Seasonal Badges

Long Beach Township is the largest of the six municipalities on Long Beach Island and has 12 miles of beach to guard and maintain—55 beaches. They are not contiguous; from the southern end of Barnegat Light to edge of the Forsythe National Wildlife Refuge in Holgate, the township's beaches are separated by the boroughs of Harvey Cedars, Surf City, Ship Bottom and Beach Haven. The beach patrol guards beaches in Loveladies, North Beach, Brant Beach (and all the Island communities to the south with the old names: Beach Haven Terrace, Crest, and Gardens; Haven Beach, Brighton Beach, The Dunes, Peahala Park, North Beach Haven, Spray Beach) as well as Holgate.

The township's beach patrol consists of nearly 200 lifeguards and almost 100 beach badge checkers — one of the largest beach patrols in the nation.

It was not until 1977 that Long Beach Township became the fifth town requiring beachgoers to purchase beach badges, eight years after Harvey Cedars and Barnegat Light began charging and a decade after Ship Bottom and Surf City.

From 1977 until 1982, the township's badges were relatively plain, changing only shape and color. From 1983 through 1989 a gull, crab, lighthouse, and sailboat were added. Then in 1990, a beach scene with an umbrella, surf, and clouds was added. With the addition of the phrase "Swim Near a Lifeguard" in 1996, and a pair of dolphins in 2003, the badges have remained fairly consistent to this day (except for the 1999 seasonal badge which, during the township's centennial celebration, was more festive.

Like many of the other towns, the township alternates the shape, color and font of its badges from year to year.

LONG BEACH TOWNSHIP
SEASONAL

TOWNSHIP LONG BEACH
SEASONAL 1978

TWP. LONG BEACH
SEASON 1979

TWP. LONG BEACH
SEASONAL 1980

TWP. LONG BEACH
SEASONAL 1981

TWP. LONG BEACH
SEASONAL 1982

TWP LONG BEACH
1983 SEASON

SEASONAL 1984
LONG BEACH TWP

LONG BEACH TWP.
1985 SEASON

19 86
TOWNSHIP OF LONG BEACH SEASON

TOWNSHIP OF LONG BEACH
SEASON

TOWNSHIP OF Long Beach
1988 SEASON

Seasonal 1989-2000

2001-2012

Township of Long Beach
Season
Swim Near A Lifeguard
2001
019340

Township of Long Beach
Season
Swim Near A Lifeguard
2002
023201

Township of Long Beach
Season
Swim Near A Lifeguard
2003
033530

Township of Long Beach
Season
Swim Near A Lifeguard
2004
017461

Township of Long Beach
2005
Season
Swim Near A Lifeguard
042449

Township of Long Beach
2006
Season
Swim Near A Lifeguard
046596

2007
Township of Long Beach
Season
Swim Near A Lifeguard
002778

2008
Township of Long Beach
Season
Swim Near A Lifeguard
030019

2009
Township of Long Beach
Season
Swim Near A Lifeguard
009760

2010
Township of Long Beach
Season
Swim Near A Lifeguard
012136

2011
Township of Long Beach
Season
Swim Near A Lifeguard
006243

2012
Township of Long Beach
Season
Swim Near A Lifeguard
036386

Seasonal 2013-2022

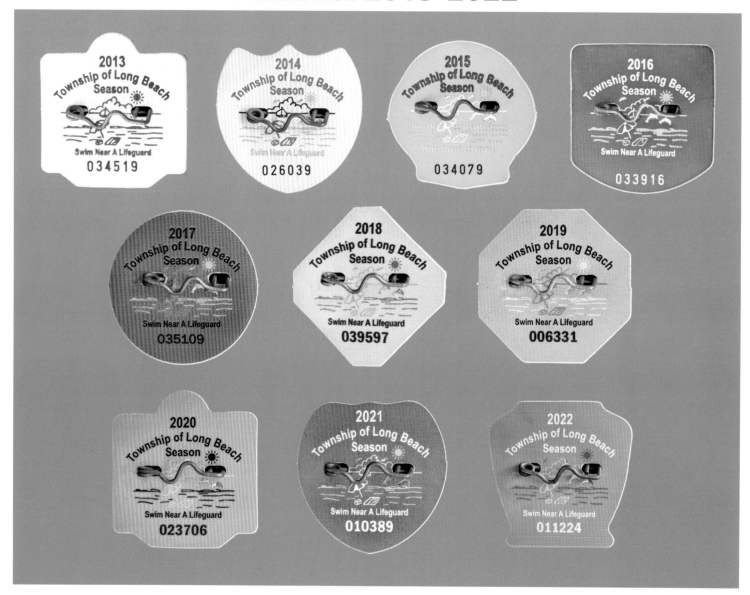

Senior Badges

A senior beach badge in the township first became available in 1986. It was a simple white badge with oars and lifebuoy design with the lettering "SCBB" (Senior Citizen Beach Badge). It was initially given out for free and was valid for life (and are still honored today). The badge changed in shape over the years and, like, the seasonal badges, a serial number was added at some point.

In 2010, senior badges were no longer free; the cost was $5 and has remained at that cost as of 2022. The badge was only valid for the year issued. While still maintaining its famililar oars, lifebuoy and serial numbers, the badges got a new look yearly, changing the shape, color and font.

One of Long Beach Twp's. first free senior badges, still valid for life.

Veteran/Military Badges

Long Beach Township offers free veteran badges with valid military ID, which are good for life. First released in 2014, the badge was tan; in 2015 the color was changed to blue. That would be the last time the year would appear on the badge, since it was good for life. Active military and their immediate family can also get free access to the beach by presenting military ID to the badge checkers.

Bayview Park Badges

In addition to the badges used by beachgoers, the township also issued Bayview Park badges, to be used at the bayside park at 68th Street for windsurfing. The badges displayed a windsurfer.

Like the other badges, the Bayview Park badges were available as seasonal, weekly and daily, and were also issued with serial numbers. The badges were issued from 1996 until 2005; prior to 1996 bumper stickers for vehicles were issued.

In 2006, these badges were no longer issued and anybody who wished to use the Bayview Park facilities could purchase the same badge as those who use the beaches.

Long Beach Twp. beach badge office, 67th. St., Brant Beach.

Senior Badges 2011-2022

Bayview Park Badges

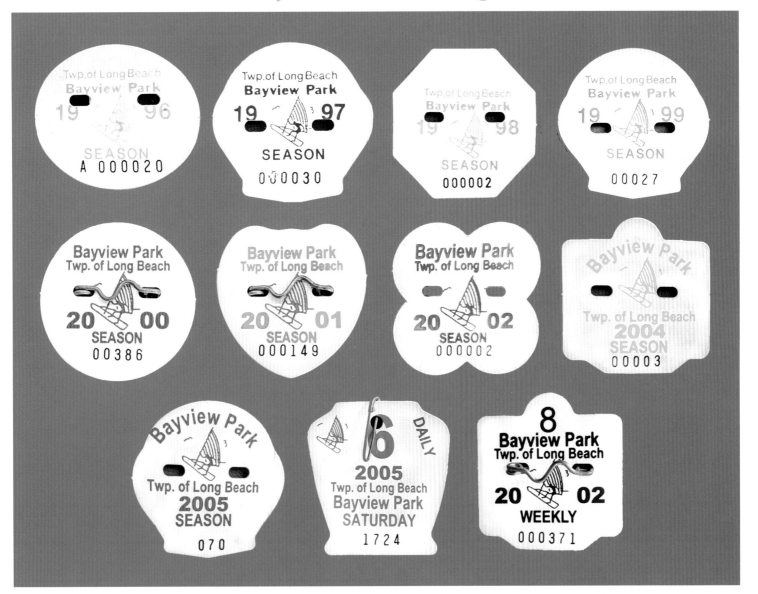

Beach Haven

Beach Badges

Beach Haven

Seasonal Badges

The borough of Beach Haven was a holdout until 1978. That year it was the last town on Long Beach Island to require bathers to purchase beach badges.

Beach Haven launched its first seasonal badge in 1978 with a sailboat as its centerpiece, but in the second year the sailboat was dropped. For most of the next quarter century the badge was plain, only changing shape, color, and type style from year to year. Then a gull was displayed in 1987, a sailboat reappeared in 1988, a whale in 1992, and two dolphins in 2000.

Nicknamed the "Queen City" since its founding in the late 19th century, the borough used a puffy crown on its badges only in 2001 and 2002. In 2003 a sailboat once again appeared as the badge icon and in the center of the badge for the next 15 years. The sailboat was gone in 2018 and replaced with dophins, a crab, a gull, a beach umbrella with chair, and a wave in the years since.

In 2011, Beach Haven started using the words "No Refund" on its seasonal badges, as well as their weekly and daily badges.

1978-1989

BEACH HAVEN, N.J.
19 78
№ .4816

BEACH HAVEN
1979
№ 5660

BEACH HAVEN
SEASONAL
1980

BEACH HAVEN
SEASONAL
1981

BEACH HAVEN
SEASONAL
1982

BEACH HAVEN
SEASONAL
1983

BEACH HAVEN
SEASONAL
1984

Beach Haven
Seasonal
1985

1986
SEASONAL
BEACH HAVEN

BEACH HAVEN
1987
SEASON

19 88
BEACH HAVEN
SEASON

BEACH HAVEN
SEASONAL
1989

Seasonal 1990-2001

BEACH HAVEN SEASONAL 1990

BEACH HAVEN 1991 Seasonal A 005531

BEACH HAVEN Seasonal 1992 A 005559

BEACH HAVEN Seasonal 1993 000382

BEACH HAVEN Seasonal 1994 A 001465

BEACH HAVEN Seasonal 1995 000895

BEACH HAVEN Seasonal 1996 A 003128

1997 BEACH HAVEN Seasonal 006371

1998 BEACH HAVEN Seasonal 008381

1999 BEACH HAVEN Seasonal 007067

BEACH HAVEN Seasonal 2000 007398

BEACH HAVEN 2001 SEASON 007021

2002-2013

BEACH HAVEN
2002
SEASON
002871

BEACH HAVEN
SEASON 2003
004033

BEACH HAVEN
SEASON 2004
009588

BEACH HAVEN
20 05
SEASON
00317

BEACH HAVEN
2006
SEASON
000328

BEACH HAVEN
2007
SEASON
004750

BEACH HAVEN
2008
SEASON
004863

BEACH HAVEN
2009
SEASON
04593

BEACH HAVEN
2010
SEASON
1565

BEACH HAVEN
2011
SEASON   NO-REFUND
10230

BEACH HAVEN
2012
SEASON   NO-REFUND
9345

BEACH HAVEN
2013
SEASON   NO-REFUND
6738

Seasonal 2014-2022

Senior Badges

Beach Haven offers a senior beach badge to those age 65 and over for a fee. Beach Haven's senior badge is a lifetime badge.

Veteran/Military Badges

Beach Haven began offering free beach badges good for life to all veterans with proper ID starting in 2014.

Beach Haven also offers free weekly wristbands to active military and their immediate family.

Beach Haven's beach badge office, on the beach at Centre St.

Beach badge checkers from 1978, the first year the borough required badges — and checkers.

TOP ROW - Left to Right:
Richard Borys, Jon Weiss, Walter Osborn-Supervisor, Barbara Crosta-Asst.Super.,
Carol Schoenberg-Asst. Super., Sally Wenal-Asst. Super., Robert Eaton,
Josh Kounitz, Charles Senior.
MIDDLE ROW - Left to Right:
Anna Grant, Diana Kleva, Kathleen Pickard, Lauren Frazer, Margaret Lyon,
Kelly Wenal, Tanya Reiner, Diane Garratt, Rosaleen Gembala.
BOTTOM ROW - Left to Right:
Christine Sprague, Barbara Pollock, Elizabeth, Claire Sieracki, Carol Price,
Liane Lipko, Trudy Russo, Heather Sirelly.
NOT PICTURED:
Beth Mania, Kurt Berger, Lorraine Wahl, Mark Becker, Edward J. Thomas,
F. "Chip" Jarczynski, Eileen Sprague, Philip Ricca, Ellen Day, Brenda Tait,
Kathleen Anderson, Marilyn Katz.

Weekly & Daily

Badges

Weekly Badges

Although not as popular, there are some collectors of beach badges who collect weekly badges as well as seasonal. Early weekly badges can be even more of a challenge to find than seasonal badges, given their brief life span.

All six towns sold weekly badges the same year they started selling seasonal badges. Some of the earliest weekly badges found are displayed on the facing page: Ship Bottom 1967, Surf City 1970, Barnegat Light 1970, Harvey Cedars 1978, Long Beach Township 1977 and Beach Haven 1979.

Over the years, there have been a number of different ways that towns used to identify their weekly badges. Some towns simply used colored coded badges; each week was represented by a different color along with the year on the badge. Some towns used a number system, weeks 1 thru 11, representing what number week of the summer it was, along with the year. Some towns used a combination of both numbers and colors. In the late '90s, Barnegat Light also included an expiration date on their weekly badges. Beach Haven in 2011, and Surf City in 2015, added the disclaimer about no refunds (as on their seasonal badges). Either way, you weren't getting your money back!

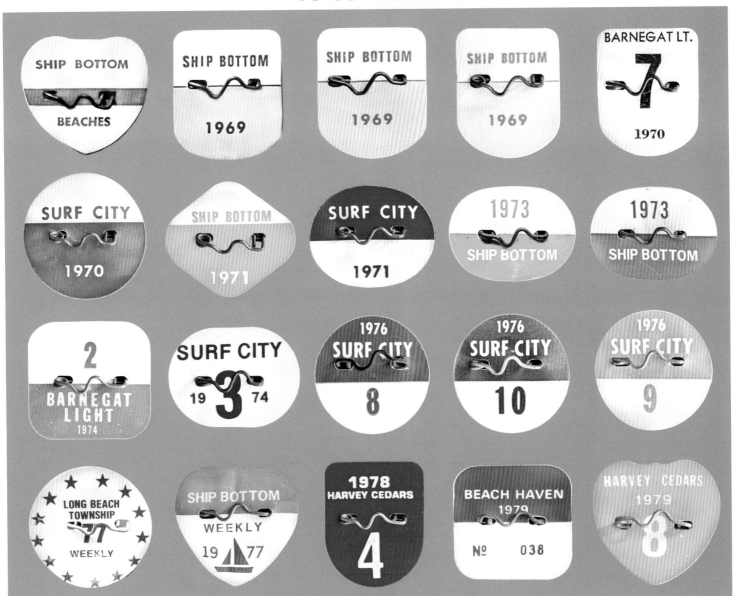

TWP. LONG BEACH 7 19 79 WEEKLY

SHIP BOTTOM WEEKLY 1980

WEEKLY 19 81 SHIP BOTTOM

9 BARNEGAT LIGHT 1982

TWP. LONG BEACH WEEKLY 19 8 82

SHIP BOTTOM WEEKLY 19 82

SHIP BOTTOM WEEKLY 19 82

SHIP BOTTOM WEEKLY 19 82

1 SURF CITY 1982

WEEKLY 1983 Harvey Cedars

WEEKLY 1983 Harvey Cedars

WEEKLY SHIP BOTTOM 19 83

3 SURF CITY 1983

1 SURF CITY 1983

LONG BEACH TWP 1 1984 WEEKLY

1984 SHIP BOTTOM WEEKLY

4 SURF CITY 1984

9 SURF CITY 1984

6 SURF CITY 1985

3 TOWNSHIP OF LONG BEACH WEEKLY 1987

1992
SURF CITY
A 00081

HARVEY CEDARS
1
1995

SHIP BOTTOM
8
WEEKLY 1995

1995
SURF CITY
7
000147

11
SURF CITY
1995
WEEKEND
A 000262

19 7 96
BARNEGAT LIGHT
WEEKLY
EXP. AUG. 10
000335

HARVEY CEDARS
9
1998

SHIP BOTTOM
WEEKLY
19 7 98
000305

BEACH HAVEN
9
19 99
000629

19 5 99
BARNEGAT LIGHT
WEEKLY
EXP. JULY 23
00113

19 11 99
BARNEGAT LIGHT
WEEKLY
EXP. SEPT. 3
00385

7
Swim Near A Lifeguard
19 99
Please Stay Off Dunes
Twp. of Long Beach
029157

SHIP BOTTOM
WEEKLY
19 99
00183

Surf City
1999
Daily/
Weekly
6
006178

20 1 00
Barnegat Light
WEEKLY
EXP. JUNE 30
000126

20 7 00
Barnegat Light
WEEKLY
EXP. AUG. 11
000065

4
Swim Near A Lifeguard
20 00
Please Stay Off Dunes
Twp. Of Long Beach
014610

SHIP BOTTOM
WEEKLY
20 7 00
000069

2002
Swim Near A Lifeguard
Please Stay Off Dunes
Twp. Of Long Beach
2
007140

2002
SURF CITY
Weekly
6
000187

Weekly 2003-2012

2003
SURF CITY
Weekly
10
001023

100th Anniversary
1904 - 2004
4
WEEKLY
Barnegat Light
EXP. JUL 16
000270

100th Anniversary
1904 - 2004
6
WEEKLY
Barnegat Light
EXP. JUL 30
000305

2004 **9** WEEKLY
Swim Near A Lifeguard
Please Stay Off Dunes
Twp. Of Long Beach
038554

9
WEEKLY
Barnegat Light
EXP. AUG. 19
2005
000405

Harvey Cedars
Week **4** 2005

Harvey Cedars
Week **7** 2005

2005 **7** WEEKLY
Swim Near A Lifeguard
Please Stay Off Dunes
Twp. Of Long Beach
32410

WEEKLY
SHIP BOTTOM
20 **4** 05
146

4
WEEKLY
Barnegat Light
EXP. JUL 14
2006
179

WEEKLY
SHIP BOTTOM
20 **6** 06
329

7 Week
Harvey Cedars
2007

10 Week
Harvey Cedars
2007

2009
BEACH HAVEN
WEEKLY
5
425

2009 **3** WEEKLY
Barnegat Light
EXP. JUL 10

2009 **6** WEEKLY
Barnegat Light
EXP. JUL 31

5 Week
Harvey Cedars
2009

HARVEY CEDARS
10

2011
SURF CITY
Weekly
4
1050

WEEKLY **1** 2012
Swim Near A Lifeguard
Please Stay Off Dunes
Twp. Of Long Beach
000759

WEEKLY **7** 2013
Swim Near A Lifeguard
015614

2013
SURF CITY
Weekly
10
1079

Week
9
Harvey Cedars
2014

WEEKLY
SHIP BOTTOM
20 **1** 15
309

WEEKLY
SHIP BOTTOM
20 **7** 15
399

2015
SURF CITY
Weekly-No Refunds
4
637

2015
SURF CITY
Weekly-No Refunds
9
120

2015
SURF CITY
Weekly-No Refunds
10
302

Week
2
Harvey Cedars
2016

Week
4
Harvey Cedars
2016

Week
8
Harvey Cedars
2016

Week
9
Harvey Cedars
2016

WEEKLY **8** 2016
Swim Near A Lifeguard
Please Stay Off Dunes
Twp. Of Long Beach
016588

WEEKLY
SHIP BOTTOM
20 **5** 16
519

2016
SURF CITY
Weekly-No Refunds
3
281

WEEKLY
SHIP BOTTOM
20 **7** 18
174

2019
SURF CITY
Weekly-No Refunds
8
1090

2020
BEACH HAVEN
WEEKLY
2
NO-REFUND
151

WEEKLY
SHIP BOTTOM
20 **9** 21
051

2021
BEACH HAVEN
WEEKLY
8
NO-REFUND
677

Weekly Collections

Harvey Cedars Weekly 2017

Week 1 Harvey Cedars 2017
Week 2 Harvey Cedars 2017
Week 3 Harvey Cedars 2017
Week 4 Harvey Cedars 2017

Week 5 Harvey Cedars 2017
Week 6 Harvey Cedars 2017
Week 7 Harvey Cedars 2017
Week 8 Harvey Cedars 2017
Week 9 Harvey Cedars 2017
Week 10 Harvey Cedars 2017
Week 11 Harvey Cedars 2017

20 **1** 00 Barnegat Light WEEKLY EXP. JUNE 30 000328

20 **2** 00 Barnegat Light WEEKLY EXP. JULY 7 000219

20 **3** 00 Barnegat Light WEEKLY EXP. JULY 14 000218

20 **4** 00 Barnegat Light WEEKLY EXP. JULY 21 000011

20 **5** 00 Barnegat Light WEEKLY EXP. JULY 28 000031

20 **6** 00 Barnegat Light WEEKLY EXP. AUG. 4 000252

20 **7** 00 Barnegat Light WEEKLY EXP. AUG. 11 000273

20 **8** 00 Barnegat Light WEEKLY EXP. AUG. 19 000464

20 **9** 00 Barnegat Light WEEKLY EXP. AUG. 25 000106

20 **10** 00 Barnegat Light WEEKLY EXP. SEPT. 1 000052

Barnegat Light Weekly 2000

WEEKLY SHIP BOTTOM 20 **1** 21 588
WEEKLY SHIP BOTTOM 20 **2** 21 533
WEEKLY SHIP BOTTOM 20 **3** 21 267

WEEKLY SHIP BOTTOM 20 **4** 21 086
WEEKLY SHIP BOTTOM 20 **5** 21 432
WEEKLY SHIP BOTTOM 20 **6** 21 547

WEEKLY SHIP BOTTOM 20 **7** 21 379
WEEKLY SHIP BOTTOM 20 **8** 21 261
WEEKLY SHIP BOTTOM 20 **9** 21 021

WEEKLY SHIP BOTTOM 20 **10** 21 091
WEEKLY SHIP BOTTOM 20 **11** 21 014

Ship Bottom Weekly 2021

Daily Badges

Harvey Cedars daily badges for 2018.

As with weekly badges, there are some collectors of daily badges. And like older weekly badges, older daily badges are more challenging to find than more current weekly badges.

Daily badges weren't offered for sale until the early '90s, when the cost of a weekly badge was becoming increasingly expensive for a one-day trip to the beach.

Over the years, towns have used a number of different ways to identify their daily badges from one day to the next. Some changed the color from day to day, some have the day of the week displayed on the badge, and some used a number or lettering system. Some towns used a combination of multiple identifiers.

Because daily badges were only needed for a short period of time (no more than eight or ten hours), early daily badges from some towns were made from a lesser quality, thinner plastic and instead of the more durable brass pin, a simple little safety pin was included for

fastening the badge onto one's bathing suit. As of 2022, only Ship Bottom and Long Beach Township still use this less expensive daily badge. Barnegat Light, Harvey Cedars, Surf City and Beach Haven have all changed to the more traditional, heavier gauge plastic with the brass pin for their daily beach badges.

In 2011 Beach Haven included the words "No Refund" (also on their seasonal and weekly badges), and in 2015 Surf City also included the words "No Refunds" on their daily badges, and similarly on their seasonal and weekly badges.

Daily 1990-2000

TUES.
19 90
SHIP BOTTOM
DAILY

SURF CITY
WEDS.
1990

FRI.
19 91
SHIP BOTTOM
DAILY

SURF CITY
19 93
MON.
A 000377

FRI.
19 94
SHIP BOTTOM
DAILY

BEACH HAVEN
19 2 95
DAILY
004347

1995
BARNEGAT
LIGHT
E
DAILY
000002

MON - 1995
SHIP BOTTOM
DAILY

SURF CITY
19 95
TUES.
000040

1996
BARNEGAT
LIGHT
A
DAILY

Swim 3 Near
A Lifeguard
19 96
Please Stay Off Dunes
Twp. of Long Beach
SUN.
12802

Swim 9 Near
A Lifeguard
19 96
Please Stay Off Dunes
Twp. of Long Beach
SAT.
039897

1997
SHIP BOTTOM
DAILY
SUN.

BEACH HAVEN
19 4 97
DAILY
000107

1998
SHIP BOTTOM
DAILY
SUN.

1999
BARNEGAT
LIGHT
G
DAILY

1999
SHIP BOTTOM
DAILY
SUN.

2000
BARNEGAT
LIGHT
E
DAILY

1
Swim Near
A Lifeguard
20 00
Please Stay Off Dunes
Twp. Of Long Beach
SUN.
001456

2000
SHIP BOTTOM
DAILY
SAT.

2000-2012

SURF CITY
2000
SUN.
000176

Swim Near A Lifeguard
20 **01**
Please Stay Off Dunes
Twp. Of Long Beach
MON.
01835

BARNEGAT LIGHT
2003
A
DAILY

Swim Near A Lifeguard
2003 **6**
Please Stay Off Dunes
Twp. Of Long Beach
TUES.
31812

SURF CITY
2003
MON.
000605

100th Anniversary
1904-2004
DAILY **F** DAILY
BARNEGAT LIGHT

2004
SHIP BOTTOM
DAILY
SAT.

SURF CITY
WED.
2005
0151

2006 **5** 2006
Swim Near A Lifeguard
Please Stay Off Dunes
Twp. Of Long Beach
SUN.
024047

SURF CITY
THUR.
2006
352

2008
BARNEGAT LIGHT
B
DAILY

2008
SHIP BOTTOM
DAILY
WED

2009
BARNEGAT LIGHT
C
DAILY

SURF CITY
2009
SAT. **12**
251

Harvey Cedars
2010
SAT.
DAILY

2010 **10** 2010
Swim Near A Lifeguard
Please Stay Off Dunes
Twp. Of Long Beach
FRI
065609

Harvey Cedars
2011
FRI.
DAILY

2011
SHIP BOTTOM
DAILY
FRI.

2012
BEACH
HAVEN
DAILY NO-REFUND
755

2012
BARNEGAT LIGHT
B
DAILY

Daily 2013-2017

2013
BEACH HAVEN
DAILY — NO-REFUND
957

2013
BARNEGAT LIGHT
H
DAILY

2013   6   2013
Swim Near A Lifeguard
Please Stay Off Dunes
Twp. Of Long Beach
MON
034517

SURF CITY
2013 MON
8
026

2014
BEACH HAVEN
DAILY — NO-REFUND
760

2014
BARNEGAT LIGHT
A
DAILY

2014
SHIP BOTTOM
DAILY
SUN

2015
BARNEGAT LIGHT
C
DAILY

2015
Harvey Cedars
TUE
DAILY

2015   3   2015
Swim Near A Lifeguard
Please Stay Off Dunes
Twp. Of Long Beach
TUE
016381

2015
SHIP BOTTOM
DAILY
MON

SURF CITY
FRI
No Refunds
2015   6
000306

2016
BEACH HAVEN
DAILY — NO-REFUND
1244

2016
BARNEGAT LIGHT
C
DAILY

2016
Harvey Cedars
SUN
DAILY

2016
SHIP BOTTOM
DAILY
SAT

SURF CITY
SUN
No Refunds
2016   6
263

2017
Harvey Cedars
WED
DAILY

2017
SHIP BOTTOM
DAILY
SUN

2017   10   2017
Swim Near A Lifeguard
Please Stay Off Dunes
Twp. Of Long Beach
SUN
065172

84

2017-2022

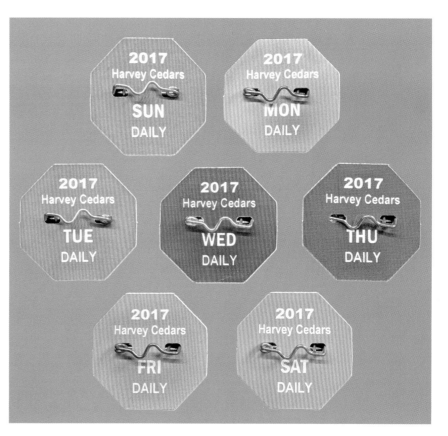

Harvey Cedars 2017 daily badge collection.

Holiday Badges

Holiday badges, sometimes referred to as the "Christmas badges," are sold by each town during the holiday season for the upcoming summer starting after Thanksgiving, depending on the town, and sold until Christmas or until these limited edition badges sell out.

Some towns offer the holiday badges in a gift box and charge an additional two dollars more than the preseason price, to cover the cost of the box.

The badges are desirable for both collectors of beach badges and for those hard to shop for beachgoers. It's a gift that's truly better than a flannel shirt.

In Ship Bottom, a holiday badge was first offered in 2011. The design of the holiday badges are the result of artwork submitted by local students from both the Long Beach Island Grade School and Ethel A. Jacobson Elementary School.

In Long Beach Township, a holiday badge was first offered in 2012. The designs are ideas from brainstorming sessions with township employees.

In Barnegat Light, holiday badges were first offered in 2012 and the design ideas are provided by borough employees.

In the Borough of Beach Haven, a holiday badge was first offered in 2014. The ideas and artwork are submitted by students from the Beach Haven School.

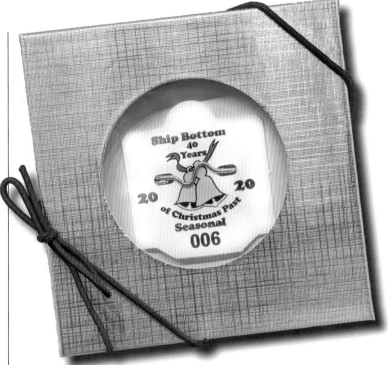

The Harvey Cedars, holiday badge was first offered in 2016 and the designs and ideas for the badge come from local students as well as Harvey Cedars own employees.

In Surf City, the holiday badge was first offered in 2017. The designs come from the several suggestion provided by the manufacturer of the badges, and then chosen by Surf City employees.

Holiday 2017-2019

2019-2022

Holiday 2022-2023

Specialty Badges

Not all badges are for the beach. Some are for private clubs, parks, and advertising. Here are just a few, including one for the St. Francis Center swim club and others for a local marina and a yacht club.

The Water's Edge was a "ma & pa" oceanfront concession on East 20th Street in Ship Bottom. It opened in the late '40s and closed in the '90s, when it was converted into a private residence.

The business included a restaurant, lockers, showers and restrooms and the badge entitled patrons — who were mostly day trippers — the use of those facilities.

This badge was found on the beach after a nor'easter had exposed it.

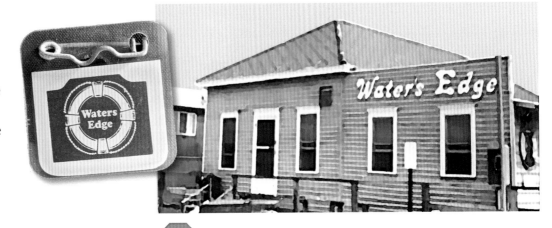

In 2006, **Starbucks Coffee,** in a promotional campaign, gave out complementary beach badges that allowed the lucky recipient a day at the beach in Long Beach Township at Starbucks's expense. At the time the coffee giant was contemplating a franchised location on Long Beach Island.

Retired beach patrol captain Don Myers remembers that the badges were handed out at several beach entrances only a few days during the summer of 2006 to anyone who would have purchased a daily badge. He added that the design came from a similar LBI Rotary Club logo.

Starbucks abandoned its Long Beach Island plans. To Starbucks lovers it was a disappointment, but for the locally owned coffee shops it was a relief.

Like many vintage badges, the Starbucks badge is extremely rare, possibly because many of the recipients were day visitors who took it home and discarded it. But for serious beach badge collectors, this badge is considered to be the Holy Grail.

Ship Bottom's volunteer fire department celebrated its 100th anniversary with this commemorative 2022 Ship Bottom seasonal badge. A portion of the proceeds from the sale of this limited edition (of 500 badges) went to the Ship Bottom Volunteer Fire Company.

The Borough of **Beach Haven** was established by the New Jersey Legislature in 1890. These limited edition seasonal badges were issued to commemorate the 125th anniversary of the borough in 2015 and its 130th anniversary in 2020. The "Queen City" gave their water tower a gold crown in the 2015 badge.

This badge was available to members of Facebook's **"LBI Beach Badge Collectors"** group where over 1100 members (as of 2022) buy, sell, trade, share stories, pictures, as well as seek and give advice about beach badges.

Where Do They Come From?

If you've ever wondered where all those beach badges come from, the answer is: Right here in the Garden State.

Jersey Cape Diagnostic, Training, and Opportunity Center, located in Cape May Court House (also known as Jersey Cape Tags) is the largest manufacturer of badges in the United States. The company manufactures 99% of the beach badges used on the Jersey Shore. In addition to beach badges made for use at the shore, they also make badges, tags and passes for lakes and pools all over the United States.

The average cost per badge to the towns is 60 cents, depending on the quantity ordered.

Established in 1973, they didn't begin manufacturing beach badges until the late '70s. On any given day there are 30-40

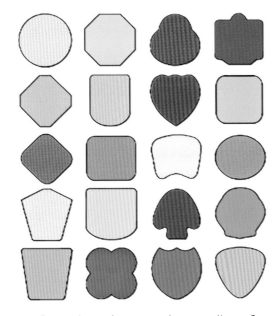

The various shapes and a sampling of the colors (ranging from "cream in my coffee" to "ocean mist") available from Jersey Cape Tags.

disabled employees who receive training from Jersey Cape Tags. These individuals assist in the assembly, packaging and delivery of the badges. With an additional 35 full time employees, the facility has the capability to work on 15 to 30 thousand badges a day, and produces roughly 4 million badges a year. The company also makes special badges for social functions, like block parties, birthday parties, and weddings.

In 2020, Jersey Cape Tags began offering a service that allowed beachgoers to purchase their seasonal badges and have them shipped, thus no more standing in line to buy beach badges. The service began with Cape May County shore communities and is expanding as more towns sign on.

Beach Badge Inflation

How prices have changed!

   Here are the costs of beach badges for Long Beach Island towns from the earliest year data is available and 2022, for comparison. (In some cases, municipalities could not provide earliest prices for all types of badges, so the price for the closest year is given.)

Surf City (began charging beach fees in 1967)

Pre-season	$17 (1999)	$35 (2022)
Seasonal	$22 "	$45 "
Weekly	$5 "	$20 "
Daily	$5 (2000)	$10 "

Ship Bottom (began charging beach fees in 1967)

Pre-season	$2 (1967)	$35 (2022)
Seasonal	$4 "	$45 "
Weekly	$1 "	$25 "
Daily	$2 (1990)	$10 "

Harvey Cedars (began charging beach fees in 1969)

Pre-season	$2 (1969)	$35 (2022)
Seasonal	$4 "	$45 "
Weekly	$1 "	$20 "
Daily	$2 (1991)	$7 "

Barnegat Light (began charging beach fees in 1969)

Pre-season	$2 (1969)	$30 (2022)
Seasonal	$4 "	$40 "
Weekly	$1 "	$22 "
Daily	$2 (1990)	$5 "

L.B. Township (began charging beach fees in 1977)

Pre-season	$2 (1977)	$35 (2022)
Seasonal	$5 (1978)	$45 "
Weekly	$2 "	$20 "
Daily	$2 (1992)	$10 "

Beach Haven (began charging beach fees in 1978)

Pre-season	$3 (1978)	$30 (2022)
Seasonal	$5 "	$40 "
Weekly	$2 "	$20 "
Daily	$2 (1992)	$10 "

About the Author

Bob Kugel grew up in Edison, NJ, but has a long history on Long Beach Island. His family's first one-week LBI vacation was in Beach Haven Gardens in 1970 when he was 13. He was hooked on the Island. Fast forward a decade, and in 1980 he owned one of the classic Holgate trailers. Four years later he bought a house in Ship Bottom. He became a full-time borough resident in 2005.

A veteran of New Jersey's telecommunications industry, he retired in 2005 and took advantage of the beach life — surf, sand, and fishing — when not doing carpentry and home improvements. He also worked from 2005 to 2022 at Southern Ocean Medical Center, which he says was "was an education about life, death, illness, medicine, and the importance of taking care of YOU." Not surprisingly, you'll find him early mornings in the gym.

He also ran a business called "Just Beach Badge Stuff" selling beach badge-themed items. Bob's daughter Lindsay has blessed him with two grandsons, Korben and Vaughn, and he looks forward to their visits at the "Kugel Kompound."

When he's not making surf art, you can find him on Facebook on his favorite LBI beach badge group, or giving online weather reports all summer long. He says without his partner Kris Kain's encouragement and push, this book would never have happened.

Acknowledgments

The author would like to thank:

Barnegat Light
Brenda L. Kuhn, Kathy VanMeter Guerrero

Harvey Cedars
Daina Dale, Anna Grimst

Surf City
Jenna Letts

Ship Bottom
Kathleen Flanagan, Kelley Nasti
Paula Bastian, Sara Dela Cruz

Long Beach Township
Renee Gresko, Danielle Lavalle

Beach Haven
Nour Khunkan

Others
Nancy Harris Taege, Richard Visotcky, Rob Burnaford
Randy David Brown, Michael Lang, Mark Vizer
Bruce McPherson, Don Myers, George Swoyer,

Photographs
page 70: Courtesy of Amanda Kaye
pages 32-33: Courtesy of Sandi Smith-Lusk

If you enjoyed this book — and for more about LBI history and culture —
you may be interested in these titles:

All Things LBI: Faves, History, Legends, Lore
ISBN 978-1-59322-106-5

Local Color: Long Beach Island's Photographic History Reimagined
ISBN 978-1-59322-124-9

Island Album: Photographs and Memories of Long Beach Island
ISBN 1-59322-087-7

The Long Beach Island Reader
ISBN 978-1-59322-095-2

Long Beach Island Chronicles
ISBN 978-1-59322-114-0

Eighteen Miles of History / Six Miles At Sea / Two Centuries of History on Long Beach Island
The classic trilogy of Long Beach Island pictorial histories by John Bailey Lloyd
ISBN 978-0-945582-17-5 / ISBN 978-0-945582-03-8 / ISBN 978-0-945582-97-7

Surviving Sandy: Long Beach Island and the Greatest Storm of the Jersey Shore
ISBN 978-1-59322-089-1

Fisherman's Wife
ISBN 978-1-59322-040-2

Down The Shore Publishing specializes in books, calendars, cards and videos
about Long Beach Island and the Jersey Shore.
Visit our website:
down-the-shore.com
Or for a catalog of all our titles just send a request: downshore@gmail.com
Down The Shore Publishing, Box 100, West Creek, NJ 08092